Night Watches

Jennifer Martin

All designwork and illustrations created by Robin Doyle.

ISBN 0-85346-191-0

Printed in Great Britain by Healeys Printers, Ipswich.

Dedication

To my beloved sister, Mary Jennings Watson, who had it in her heart to use her pen for the Lord, but instead was called to go and share His glory.

Thanks

My grateful thanks to my dear friend Mrs Muriel Palmer, without whose loving encouragement and advice this book would not have been written.

Also my gratitude goes to Scripture Union, and its workers, who through Bible Study notes, school's work, books and Junior Church material, have consistently ministered to my Christian faith for the last forty five years.

Introduction

This little book contains a series of meditations based on stories, and on images of God, which we find in the Bible. In each one we are encouraged to use the mind's eye to unpack the story or image so that it might travel from the head to the heart, and in so doing feed our whole being.

The meditations are useful, for corporate or personal devotion, in church or on retreat or at any other quiet time in the day.

Their original inspiration was, however, as meditations for use when it was difficult to sleep so they can also be used before going to sleep in the evening, or in periods of wakefulness during the night. The Pslamist says 'On my bed I remember you; I think of you during the night. Because you are my help, I sing in the shadow of your wings.' Psalm 63v6. Because you may be using these meditations like this, I have deliberately chosen subjects for meditation which encourage us to see God as a loving caring force, but we must not forget the other more challenging side to the gospel message, of sin, forgiveness and witness. In a particularly difficult period of my life, I found such meditation a life line. I hope it will be the same for you. May this book be a blessing to all who use it in the day and a source of peace and comfort to those who suffer in the watches of the night.

A Breathing Prayer

This is a little prayer you can repeat over and over
again as you quietly rest in God's presence.
I am with you Lord Jesus.

Prayer

Lord Jesus, as I look into your radiant face, I feel my
fears and doubts shrink to their proper size. You are
here, with me now, and I can never be outside your
care and love. As a little child rests in the secure
presence of its mother or father even so I rest my
whole body and soul in your infinite care.

Amen.

When I awake I shall be satisfied with seeing your likeness.
Psalm 17: 15

To understand what the Psalmist is saying about our Father God in this verse, you must imagine that you are a child again. Your mother is putting you to bed. She sits on your bed and tells you a good night story. Then you both close your eyes whilst she prays with you. Perhaps then, you snuggle down to sleep to the sound of her voice as she sings a quiet lullaby.

The last thing you see before you close your eyes is her face bending over you full of love and concern just for you alone. Gradually you begin to feel sleepy until her voice fades and you are in a beautiful, restful, refreshing sleep.

Morning comes and it is time to get up. Your mother comes to waken you. She bends over and kisses you and you open your eyes to look into the same loving face you saw before you fell asleep. All is well with the world and you feel secure and safe in the knowledge that she is there and with you.

Now go through the sequence outlined above again, only this time see yourself as an adult, going to bed. Imagine the face of Jesus bending over you as you close your eyes. Think through the hours of night with Him by your bed watching over you in a way even your mother could not have done. Then imagine waking in the morning and the first thing you see as you open your eyes is His face, full of the utmost tenderness and love looking down on you. Feel the joy that the sight brings to your whole being.

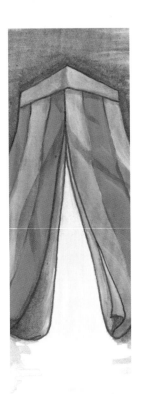

Breathing Prayer

In the middle of the storm we are together Lord.

Prayer

Trouble comes Lord Jesus, and I feel threatened and overwhelmed. What I would really like to happen is for the trouble to be taken away from me, and that all my life should become smooth and easy. But I know this will never happen. So when I'm up against it Lord, help me to find a secret place of safety in your loving presence.

Amen.

For in the day of trouble He will keep me safe in His dwelling; He will hide me in the shelter of his tabernacle [this can also be translated pavilion or tent] and set me high upon a rock. **Psalm 27 v 5**

Imagine, that you are walking through a desolate countryside. Your path leads you up a rocky path between high craggy hills. Wind-stunted bushes and cushions of rough grass are the only vegetation. Dark clouds are rolling in, filling the sky-space over-head and you stop to put your waterproof on. Soon the rain comes and the wind. You put your head down to see where you are going.

You struggle round a bend in the path, and there, a few feet from the track is a rocky outcrop forming a small area of flat ground. On this, an Eastern-style tent is pitched. It looks low and black, as it crouches there weathering the storm. As you hesitate, the entrance cover is drawn aside and a hand beckons you in.

You stoop down and enter. The entrance cover falls behind you and the sound of the storm is muted. Inside, the tent is beautifully appointed with cush-ions and carpets. You take off your waterproof and feel warmth and security all around you. A meal is laid out on a low table. You eat, and then lie down on a low couch. The storm still rages out-side, but in here all is warm and safe. You fall asleep.

God is like this tent in the storm. He is a safe place in time of trouble.

Breathing Prayer

When I least expect it Lord, you are there.

Prayer

Lord Jesus I am amazed that you should make time in
your eternal schedule to come and comfort one small
insignificant human being in her distress. I can see that
her grief was important to you and that encourages my
faith. I can also see that you love me in the same way,
and that my joys and sorrows are equally significant.
Thank you Lord, of your care for Mary, and thank you
for your care for me.

Amen.

This meditation is centred on the well-known story of Jesus' appearance to Mary after the resurrection.

Imagine you are in a garden. It is early dawn, and the sky is just beginning to pale. It's cold. Behind you is the blackness of several tall trees, but in front the ground slopes down steeply to a gravelled area. At the back of this looms a small cliff about twenty feet high. The light is just sufficient to pick out the eye-brow-fringe of rough grass on its summit, silhouetted against the pale sky and stars. Outlined in the cliff base is the round hole of Jesus' tomb. It's not black and dark but faintly luminous.

As you watch, a figure stumbles out of the tomb entrance. It's Mary, in deep distress. She is crying and seems unable to see around her. Just then a figure appears out of the shadow, and a gentle voice says 'Dear lady, why are you crying?' With head still bowed, she replies, 'If you took him away sir, tell me where you have put him and I will go and get him.' Somehow you feel an eternal weight of sorrow in these stumbling words.

Then in tones of utmost consolation you hear one word spoken in reply - 'Mary.' There is an instant's electric joy before Mary throws her-self at Jesus' feet. Again comes the warm, gentle voice. 'Do not hold on to me, because I have not yet gone back up to the Father. But go to my brothers and tell them that I am returning to him who is my Father and their Father, My God and their God.' Wave upon wave of radiant joy seem to flow from Mary to you as she hears these words. You follow her with your eyes until she has run out of the garden. You turn to look for Jesus, but He has gone. Over the tomb the sky has changed to pale yellow. The dawn has come.

Breathing Prayer

Praise you Jesus for my heavenly home.

Prayer

Lord Jesus I can't wait to join your sons and
daughters as they come home to you. I can hear
the singing and feel the joy as their feet near your
Holy City. It would be convenient to skip the next
bit of life here on earth and go straight on to the
party Lord, but I know that is not possible. So,
please give me the strength to carry on, secure in
the knowledge that I shall indeed one day be part
of your joyful heavenly host.

Amen.

*Please read **Isaiah ch 35**. This chapter can be inter-
preted as the return of the Jewish exiles from Babylon, or
as a description of the road by which the pilgrims of all
nations shall journey to God's holy Mount Zion.*

You are standing on the edge of a vast and formless
desert. As far as you can see are lifeless sand dunes
and parched rock. Over this silent scene the sun
burns down and the heat is unbearable. The whole
picture is desolate and forsaken.

As you watch the sand and rock begins to heave, like
a giant gently shaking himself. A green line advances
across the desert from your feet to the horizon. It's
grass. Up through the earth flowers grow as in a
speeded-up film and lastly trees burst from the
ground and arch here and there giving the scene a
park-like effect. Then you hear a noise you
recognise, that of cascading water. You turn, and
there nearby flows a stream. When you turn again,
you are amazed to see that a lake fringed by tall
reeds has appeared in the middle distance.

You glance at your feet and note that they are
standing on the stone blocks of a wide road. Slowly
you lift your eyes and see that the road unwinds on
and on until in the distance you can see the towers
and sparkling palaces of a beautiful city.

Behind you, you hear the sound of rushing
feet and wild, joyful singing. A crowd surges
past you, singing and shouting for joy. Their
ecstasy is infectious and you watch them as
they leap and dance their way along the
road until at last the great gates of the city
are opened and they pass inside.

One day, you realise, you will join them.

Breathing prayer

Save me from myself Oh Lord.

Prayer

My self will and my sin must grieve you Lord Jesus.
How much you wanted to take your own people and
shield them from others and from themselves. How sad
you must have been when they refused you. Help me,
never to be like them. May I run to the shelter of your
wings in time of trouble. Shield me from my foolish
actions. For your name's sake.

Amen.

*Dear Jesus, as a hen covers her chicks with her wings, to
keep them safe, do Thou this dark night protect us under
your golden wings.*
A prayer from India from 'Another Day'
compiled by John Carden, published by Triangle.

Jesus said 'Jerusalem, Jerusalem! You kill the prophets, you stone the messengers God has sent you! How many times have I wanted to put my arms round all your people, just as a hen gathers her chicks under her wings, but you would not let me!'
Luke 13 v 34

Imagine what it would feel like to be a very small chick! Your arms have become little embryonic wings, your legs little stick-like appendages with claws on the bottom. And most peculiar of all, you can only see in one dimension and that on either side of you. Instead of skin, you have bright yellow down.

You are very curious and go scrapping here and there looking for food, but also interested in any new object that comes within the vision of either of your eyes. You peck it, to see whether it is good to eat or not.

Behind you in a barred coop is your mother hen. You can hear her clucking caution to you but you take no notice. Then you hear an unfamiliar sound and look up. There towering above you is the farmer. Behind you your mother's quiet clucking has become a loud danger call and you turn back, run into the coop and dive beneath her wings.

Once under her wings you feel warm and safe. The feathers are soft and dark and you can forget the fearsome sight of the farmer who represents an imagined danger to you both. You tuck your legs under you, put your head in your own little wings and go to sleep. Even so would God take and shield us, not only from the things which would harm us but from our own stupidity.

Breathing Prayer

Your promises Lord are my security.

Prayer

Lord God, I marvel at your graciousness, that you
came to comfort deceitful Jacob and assure him of
your presence. He certainly didn't deserve such
love, or such a beautiful vision of the side door into
Heaven. But I too resemble Jacob more closely than
I would care to admit and so I take heart that You
are nearer to me than I can possibly begin
to understand.

Amen.

Though, like the wanderer, [Jacob] the sun has
gone down,
Darkness be over me, my rest a stone;
Yet in my dreams I'd be nearer, my God, to Thee,
Nearer to Thee!
[Sarah Flower Adams, Congregational Praise]

If you are not familiar with the story of Jacob and Esau, their fight over the elder brother's birthright, and Jacob's subsequent flight, you will find them in
Genesis chs 27 and 28.

In your mind's eye, see Jacob, come out of this tent, kiss his mother goodbye and set off with his bundle of provisions on the long journey away from home. How sad he looks. Follow him as he travels that first day, through the rugged terrain of Palestine.

At last the sun begins to set behind the craggy hills and you watch Jacob as he looks around for somewhere to camp. There are no houses near by and dejectedly he rolls himself in his cloak, puts his head on a most uncomfortable-looking stone pillow, and falls asleep. The night gathers round him and the stars come out. It is dark.

Imperceptibly the darkness around the lonely figure begins to lighten. You can begin to trace a faintly glowing outline. Soon you see that you are looking at a beautiful golden stairway, leading from where Jacob is lying, up into the vastness of the heavens. As your eyes become accustomed to the dazzling light of the stairway, you see that there are even more dazzling figures going up and down it. These appear to be angelic beings.

Then, awesome, beyond belief, you sense that the presence of God is standing next to Jacob and you hear Him say to Jacob 'Remember, I will be with you and protect you wherever you go, and I will bring you back to this land. I will not leave you until I have done all that I have promised you.' The words bring comfort to your own heart also and you are left in silent contemplation of this pathway to heaven in the wilderness.

Breathing Prayer

Little Jesus, be my Lord.

Prayer

I have often wanted to be at the stable where you were born, Lord Jesus. I too would have worshipped you and marvelled at all that eternity done up in so small a bundle. It was a wonderful plan Lord, and I am so glad to be a part of it even though only a small one. May I never forget your sacrifice in coming into the world to save me.

Amen.

The story of the shepherds at Christ's birth is well known, but if you want to check the facts you will find them in **Luke ch 2vvs 8 - 20**

The air is crisp and cold. You are sitting on a bleak hillside with some shepherds. A little fire burns nearby, a centre of warmth and comfort. In the distance, you can see one or two little lights twinkling and you know that in that direction is the town of Bethlehem, clinging to the side of a rocky escarpment. Taste the sharp, cold air and listen to the night sounds.

Suddenly, with no warning, the sky is lit up with an unearthly radiance and a mighty figure at the centre of the light speaks to you. 'Don't be afraid! I am here with good news for you, which will bring great joy to all the people. This very day in David's town your Saviour was born - Christ the Lord! And this will prove it to you; you will find a baby wrapped in swaddling clothes and lying in a manger.'

The radiant light enfolds you and the sound of angels winging breaks in upon your ears. You are wrapped in awe and amazement. The sky darkens, the vision fades and silence falls. Then every one begins to talk at once as you discuss what has happened. As one man, you decide to go and see for yourself if what the angel has said is true.

Imagine your journey. It would take about an hour. First over rough ground then nearer the escarpment, over the field that once belonged to Ruth and Boaz, and lastly the back-breaking climb up the twisting track to the town. Once at the inn a hubbub of sounds and smells and busy people engulfs you. Then you are led to the stable. The door is opened and you peer hesitantly inside. Yes, it's a stable all right, but the amongst all the mess, in the dim flickering interior, sits a young woman with a tiny scrap of humanity in her arms. There in, a palpable atmosphere of awe, you worship.

Breathing Prayer

Hear your Heavenly Father whisper to your spirit,
'You are more precious to me than all the flowers I
have made.'

Prayer

The beauty of your flowers Lord God, constantly fills
me with delight. I love their colours, their shapes
and scents. And yet you lavish all this beauty on
things that only last for a little while. How much
more must You love me Lord. I must trust You more
and more each day to care for me too.

Amen.

Look how the wild flowers grow: they do not work or make clothes for themselves. But I tell you that not even King Solomon with all his wealth had clothes as beautiful as one of these flowers. It is God who clothes the wild flowers,....won't he be all the more sure to clothe you?
Matthew ch 6 vvs 28 - 30.

Come with me for a walk in an imaginary garden. It's a beautiful garden, with smooth lawns, shady walks and an abundance of flowers. We choose a path at random, and explore. The path rounds a bend and we come face to face with a tall sunflower. We stop and admire its dark centre jammed with seeds, and its glorious fringe of sunshine yellow petals. We see the strength of the stem and the complementary green leaves.

Our way then takes us over a lawn spangled with daisies. We sit under the shade of an overarching tree, and pick one. Again we wonder at the bright yellow centre of the daisy and marvel at the many tiny petals, shading away from palest pink to purest white.

A rose garden comes next and on each bush there is a profusion of beautiful blooms. One in particular catches our eye. It is a deep velvet red and has half opened. Inside the petals is a single drop of dew, which catches the sun and sparkles like crystal. The petals themselves have a soft, silky feel to the touch, and are rolled round each other in perfect symmetry.

At last we come to the garden's edge. There the ground falls away, and we gaze down a gentle hill. The hill is covered in corn, and in amongst the corn are myriads of poppies. In fact the field appears to have been washed with crimson. We stand and drink in this beautiful sight.

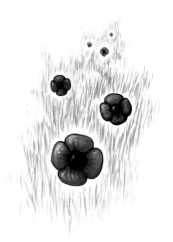

And yet, God, who has painted each individual flower from great to small, loves us infinitely more than these parts of His creation on which He has lavished such astounding beauty.

If you have a favourite walk you can retrace in your mind, or a flower or plant you can look at, try that as a variation.

Breathing Prayer

Feed me Lord Jesus

Prayer

Lord Jesus, the provisions you provided for the five
thousand were very basic - bread and fish.
Doubtless some of them would have preferred a few
luxuries, like a handful of grapes and a slice or two of
cheese. But you knew that your food was more
than adequate to get them home that night. Help
me to trust You to supply, not my wants,
but my needs.

Amen.

The miracle of the feeding of the five thousand people is well known. The details may be found in **Mark ch 5 vvs 33 - 44.**

For most of the day the sun has been warm on your back, but now it has moved round to start its slow decline behind the craggy hills across the beautiful Lake of Galilee. All day you have been watching and listening to Jesus preaching. [You might like to fill in some of the things you would have heard and seen from your knowledge of the Gospel story] Next to you on a large boulder sits a young lad. He has been so enthralled that his lunch, tied up in a cloth, has remained uneaten.

You hear the disciples ask Jesus to send the people away, and Jesus' reply, telling them to see how much food the people have left. A disciple comes towards you and the lad jumps off the boulder and shyly offers his meal. You follow their progress to Jesus. Jesus looks down at the lad, and gravely takes the meagre provisions. There is a stirring in the crowd like the whisper of wind over a corn field as they all sit down. You watch, captivated, as Jesus takes a little loaf in his hands, looks up to His Father, God, and asks a blessing. Then He breaks it, and puts the pieces into an out-stretched basket. Again and again He does this, and yet there is no end to the bread and the fish. When a basket of food is held out to you by one of the disciples, you wonderingly take from it and eat. You are hungry, so it tastes doubly deli-cious for this is the food of a miracle. As the last rays of the sun slant across the lake, you watch the disciples moving over the hillside collecting up an amazing twelve baskets full of scraps. Night falls and you return with a multitude of wondering people to your village.

Breathing Prayer

Light of the world, shine on me.

Prayer

Lord Jesus, light of the world, come into my heart,
and light up the dark places there. Fill me with your
pure radiance so that all that belongs to the dark
may melt away and be lost, never to return. As a
sunflower follows the sun, may my desire always be
towards you.

Amen.

Jesus said, 'I am the light of the world, whoever follows me will have the light of life, and will never walk in darkness.'
Goods News, John ch 8 v 12.

The light shines in the darkness, and the darkness has never put it out. **Good News, John ch 1 v 5.**

You are standing on a hill overlooking a broad cultivated plain. It's a windy day and the clouds are jostling across the heavens. All is dull and dreary. Suddenly a break in the clouds appears, and the sun begins to light up the far edge of the plain. As the wind continues to blow, the sun patch quickly spreads, until all the scene is bathed in sunshine. Transforming light has come, and with it gladness and serenity.

Again, imagine that you are in a completely dark room. You can see nothing at all. As you strain your eyes, you think you can see a faint glow just in front of you. As you watch, the outline of a candle flame appears flickering dimly. Shadows begin to play on the walls of the room as the candle flame gets brighter and brighter. At last it is so bright that it fully illuminates the room. All the darkness has been banished. You are conscious of that it is still indeed dark outside, but this super-bright candle, you are sure, has the strength to keep it forever at bay.

Imagine you are sitting on the deck of a liner just before the dawn breaks. You can hear the waves, and the darkness is all around you. As you wait, cuddled up in a blanket, there is an almost imperceptible lightening of the sky. You watch carefully and second by second the sky becomes paler until you see the sun rise over the sea, making a radiant pathway and turning all to gold. Day has again triumphed over night.

Breathing Prayer

Glorious Lord, breathe your fragrance into my soul.

Ivory Palaces

My Lord has garments so wondrous fine,
And myrrh their texture fills,
Their fragrance reached to this heart of mine,
With joy, my being thrills.

Out of the Ivory Palaces, into a world of woe,
Only his great eternal love, made my Saviour go.
[H. Barraclough. 1915. Taken from Crusader Hymns,
copyright 1966 Hope Publishing Co. Chicago,
Illinois 60644]

All your robes are fragrant with myrrh and aloes and cassia; from palaces adorned with ivory the music of the strings makes you glad. **Psalm 45:8**

The presence of Jesus has long been associated with a beautiful perfume.

Imagine you are in an arbour in a beautiful garden. Outside the arbour is a pool with a small fountain playing. You are sitting on a seat and in front of you is a table with four different herbs laid out on it. First you take up a sprig of Rosemary and crushing its spiky leaves, smell its astringent perfume. Then you turn to a posy of Lavender. Thirdly you inhale the refreshing aroma of Lemon Balm and, lastly, the aromatic scent of bruised Mint leaves tickles your nose. [Put in your own favourite herbs or spices]

You rise and go to the doorway of the arbour. There you stop and inhale deeply the beautiful perfume of the Honeysuckle with which it is surrounded. It's early evening and its delicate scent is all pervasive. With the music of the fountain in your ears, you pass under a stone archway into a formal garden of Roses. The borders are sown with Night-Scented Stock and the perfume of Rose and Stock
mingles on the evening air.

You linger here, eyes closed savouring the all-pervading loveliness. At last you bend your footsteps toward the house and your bedroom. You get into your bed [make this as comfortable as you can!] and turn out the light. One last delight awaits you for as you drift off to sleep, you are surrounded by the glorious scent of a large bowl of sweetpeas on your bedside table.

None on these scents can compare with the glorious perfume of our King in His splendour.

Breathing Prayer

Work on my life, to your glory.

Prayer

Lord Jesus, you have begun to fashion out of the raw
material of my life, the person you want me to be.
Give me patience to wait until that work is
complete. May each experience of life, whether
pleasant or difficult, be a chisel in your hand to
create something of final beauty.

Amen.

Let us fix our eyes on Jesus, the author and perfecter of our faith, who for the joy set before him endured the cross, scorning its shame, and sat down at the right hand of the throne of God.
Hebrews 12:2

The image here can be seen as that of a sculptor, who not only conceives the sculpture, but takes the project through to completion.

You are sitting in a stone mason's yard. In front of you is a large block of marble, lumpy and angular. As you watch, the sculptor arrives, takes hammer and chisel, and begins to chip away at the marble. The chippings fly in all directions. Every now and again, the sculptor stops, steps back and thinks about the form imprisoned in the stone.

Each day you go back and watch him at work. After some time you dimly see the outline of a kneeling figure beginning to emerge from the marble. It appears to have its hands upraised in joy or ecstasy.

Weeks pass and still you haunt the yard. Patiently the sculptor works away at the figure. One day, when he has gone home you go very close to the stone figure and discover to your astonishment that the sculpture is of you. The face is yours and on it is an expression of spine-tingling worship. However the rest of the figure is still rough-hewn.

When you go back the next day, the sculptor seems to be beginning on a new phase of work. Each part is worked over again and fine details of dress and features are painstakingly put in.

Is this all? No, the final phase comes when the figure is polished until it shines. There, in all its perfection, is a statue of you, beautiful in every detail and in an attitude of perfect worship.

Breathing Prayer

Jesus, I love you too!

Prayer

Lord Jesus, you shared that lovely meal with your
disciples by the quiet lakeside. What a privilege they
had, to have you serve their food, and to see you
sitting by the fire caring for them. Make me quiet,
deep inside Lord, so that I too may be aware of your
presence with me, caring for me and loving me as
you cared for and loved your first friends.

Amen.

This meditation is based on Jesus' appearance to his seven disciples after His resurrection and can be found in **John ch 21.**

DAY THIRTEEN

You are standing in amongst the bushes which fringe a small cove on the Sea of Galilee. There is a tiny beach in front of you and on it stands Jesus, looking out over the water. Across the lake you can see the day beginning to dawn over the far mountains. Beside Jesus is a small charcoal fire on which are cooking several fish. Nearby are some loaves of bread.

As you look out over the lemon-coloured sea, you see the dark silhouette of a fishing boat. It comes nearer until it is within hailing distance. Jesus shouts to the boat. 'Young men, haven't you caught anything?' 'Not a thing' comes back the reply. 'Then throw your net out on the right side of the boat, and you will catch some.' There's a splash and out goes the net. You can see the figures in the boat struggling with it to try and get it back on board. Then another splash as Peter leaps into the water and comes racing ashore.

How does he greet Jesus? Does he fall at his feet? Or does he just stand amazed and overawed at the sight of his beloved master? Slowly the boat edges into land and the other disciples come shyly towards the fire. 'Go and get some of the fish' Jesus commands, and Peter hurries off and drags the net, single-handed up the tiny beach.

Very gently Jesus says 'Come and eat' and when they have sat down, He shares with them, first bread and then the fish from the fire. You watch entranced as breakfast begins and as the sun's rays trace a path of gold to the little cove you strain your ears to hear the conversation. 'Simon, son of John, do you love me?' 'Lord, you know everything, you know that I love you.' 'Feed my sheep and my lambs,' says Jesus' quiet voice and it falls on your ears like a benediction.

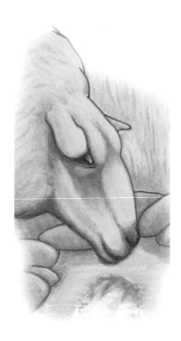

Breathing Prayer

Rested, led, restored.

Prayer

Lord Jesus, the picture of you as my shepherd is a very precious one. I like to think of you guiding me into the places that You want me to go. Where You find rest for me, there I would lie down, and my soul is ever in need of being restored. May I follow your leading without question and never stray from your company. Fold me tonight [today] in the strong arms of your protecting presence.

Amen.

He makes me lie down in green pastures, he leads me
beside quiet waters, he restores my soul.
Psalm 23:2

I wonder what it feels like to be a sheep. To have a leg
at each corner and a woolly coat? If you can perform
this feat of imagination, put yourself in the corner of a
sunny field in early Spring. Behind you is a hedgerow,
just beginning to burst into leaf. Primroses and violets
scent the air, and the fresh new grass is awash with
daisies. Lying comfortably in lush meadow must, for a
sheep, be rather like being in the middle of a free,
well-stocked supermarket or restaurant. It's all there
for the taking. All you have to do is eat it, and then sit
in the pleasant sunshine, out of the wind and chew,
whilst the earthy smell of Spring drifts all around you.

When you become thirsty, you amble down the sloping
hillside, to a stream that runs in the valley. At this point
the stream widens out into a pool. The water is still
and brown under a canopy of branches. Small fish swim
in its depths and the bank shelves gently down. You
stand by the water in the shade of the trees, your
reflection shadowy and dim in its cool depths.

How is your soul restored? What is it you
need most at the moment? If it is peace,
experience it flowing into your body and mind
filling every sore and hurt place. Perhaps it is
not peace but courage you need. Feel the
courage of the Good Shepherd filling all the
frightened places in your life. Or maybe you
need to feel His forgiveness washing over you,
taking all the long-held guilt and remorse and
sending it away for ever. Quietly stay in His
company, gentled by His love and held in His
reassuring presence.

Breathing Prayer

Your power, Your energy.

Prayer

You have done some surprising things Lord, but this
is one of the most surprising. First the two disciples
thought they were with a total stranger, and then, in
a twinkling, they knew it was You. Perhaps you are
just as apparent to me now but my eyes, like theirs,
can only see the obvious. Open them Lord, that I
may grasp that You are indeed here and sharing my
life too.

Amen.

They asked each other, 'Were not our hearts burning within us while he talked with us on the road and opened the Scriptures to us?'
Luke 24:32
[The whole story of the two disciples' meeting with Jesus can be found in ch 24 of Luke's gospel.]

Close your eyes. Now open them on the window of your mind and see yourself standing on a rocky road in the high Judean hills. A little way ahead are three people, Jesus, Cleopas and Cleopas's wife. You catch them up and listen as Jesus expounds the Old Testament Scriptures. The two disciples are clearly captivated and puzzled all at the same time.

The little party comes to the turn-off for Emmaus. Jesus looks as if He is going further but the other two insist He comes to their house. Once inside, Mrs Cleopas bustles around putting out the food they have brought with them from Jerusalem; bread, perhaps cheese, raisins and water to drink. The room is filled with the shadows of impending night as the three sit round the low table on the floor.

'You ask a blessing' says Jesus and the two disciples begin to bow their heads. Jesus takes the bread, and in one oh-so-familiar movement, breaks it and begins to say words they have heard Him say a thousand times. The two stare at Him in wonder, and then suddenly He is not there any more.

'Wasn't it like a fire burning in us when He talked to us on the road and explained the Scriptures to us,' they say to each other and their faces are full of radiant joy. With new-found energy they rush off back the long road to Jerusalem and the other disciples.

Breathing prayer

Carried on Your wings.

Prayer

I like to think of You shielding me and caring for me
like that parent eagle, Lord. Not stopping me from
falling but, like the eagle, encouraging me to have a
go at some new and difficult thing. And then when I
get into difficulties, being there to scoop me up on
your powerful wings and urge me on until I start
again. Thank you for the power of Your protection.

Amen.

He shielded him and cared for him; he guarded him as the apple of his eye, like an eagle that stirs up its nest and hovers over its young, that spreads its wings to catch them and carries them on its pinions.
Deuteronomy 32:11
[This is not a meditation to be done by anyone who is afraid of heights!]

You are sitting high up on a wide ledge in a beautiful mountain range. The air is pure and cold and far below you, you can see the valley floor. Houses look like toys, and fields and rivers like a child's farm. Immediately below is a smaller ledge and on it is an eagle's nest with one small eagle in it. He is all alone and sitting in imperious state staring out at the far mountain peaks. As you marvel at the view you hear a rush of wings and see a fully-grown eagle wheeling and turning in the sky. You watch, and with an incredible display of split-second timing, it lands on the ledge beside the egret.

Fascinated, you observe the parent gently push the fledgling off the ledge into the abyss. The small bird flutters bravely, but can't seem to get the hand of how to fly and begins to fall. In an instant the parent bird is there underneath, and with wings outstretched it catches the baby bird and brings it back to the safety of the nest.

Again it pushes the little one of the edge, and again rescues it when it gets into difficulties. At last, and after much practice, the little eagle begins to master the basic mechanics of flight, and comes and goes at will, to and from the ledge. Even so, the parent bird keeps a watchful eye on the practice flights, and is ready at any moment for another mid-air rescue.

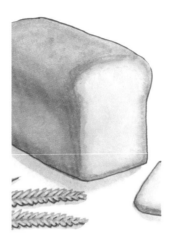

Breathing prayer
Sustaining God.

Prayer
Lord God, without your wonderful provision of
bread the lives of many of your children would end.
Thank you for it and thank you too that Jesus
sustains my spiritual life in the same sort of way.
May I ever be aware that just as I have to eat my
bread for it to do me any good, even so I must be at
one with Jesus for Him to give me life.

Amen.

Then Jesus declared, 'I am the bread of life. He who comes to me will never go hungry, and he who believes in me will never be thirsty.'
John 6:35

Bread! Can you make it? If you have made bread in the past you will remember the feel of the flour in the bowl as you mix it round with your hand, and the smell of the yeast, sugar and warm water will be an odour never to be forgotten. The biggest fun in bread-making is the kneading however. Imagine you are kneading your dough now, pummelling it and folding it back on itself until the outer layer cracks. Then press it into the tin and leave it in a warm place. An hour later, there it is, miraculously risen to twice its size. Soon the smell of baking bread is all over the house. Then comes the magic moment when you take it out of the oven and turn the loaf out to cool. And the even better moment when you cut the first slice and savour the texture and flavour of your own bread.

Now call to mind the shelves of bread in the supermarket. See the sandwich loaves, the cottage loaves, the bloomers, and the sliced bread. Also the little rolls in all shapes and sizes, from the small crusty variety to large and floury baps. How many mouths will this amount of bread feed? How many hunger pangs will it assuage. If bread were like petrol, and humans did miles to the gallon, how many miles would the human body run on this much bread? And how many fields of golden corn had to be harvested to provide the flour for this many loaves? Visualise the two side-by-side, the field of corn and the shelves laden with so many different varieties of bread. Let a feeling of thankfulness sweep over you at God's marvellous provision, and His acted parable.

Breathing Prayer

I trust You, my provider.

Prayer

Lord, how Jacob must have longed to hear that
Joseph was alive, yet when he was told the news by
his sons he could hardly believe it. It took the
thoughtful provision of practical travelling
arrangements to convince him of the truth. May I
too, Lord, provide practical love and help to your
children, and so convince them of your love and
reality. May I be your Joseph to those in need.

Amen.

But when they told him all that Joseph had said to them, and when he saw the wagons which Joseph had sent to take him to Egypt, he recovered from the shock. **Genesis 45:27**
[You can find the story of Joseph in the preceding chapters of Genesis]

Take a low flight over the barren hills of Judah in the time of the patriarchs. You come upon a shallow valley and down below you see a collection of tents and a small crowd of people. Away over the valley's edge a line of ox carts is slowly making its laborious way along the track, leading to the encampment.

Landing, you join the crowd, and find that at the centre is an old, old man who is in heated conversation with a group of younger men. They appear to have just come into camp for many tired donkeys loaded with sacks of grain are standing patiently waiting to be unloaded.

The old man, whose name is Jacob, says 'I don't believe it. You can't possibly have seen my son Joseph. He is dead.' He shakes his head in a bewildered and exhausted way. 'But he's not dead' replies one of the young men, Jacob's sons. 'We saw him. We talked to him and we even ate with him. What can we do to make you believe us?'

Just then, a low rumbling sound is borne in upon the little crowd and they all turn round to stare up the track that leads to the valley's rim. Jacob too peers into the distance. At last over the edge comes the lead wagon, with the oxen straining from the climb. At a faster pace, it descends and comes to rest in front of Jacob. 'What is the wagon for?' he asks querulously. 'Those are the wagons Joseph has sent to take you to Egypt' replies one of the sons. Light begins to dawn on Jacob's face like sunshine chasing the shadows away. 'Then Joseph is alive' he breathes. 'I will go to him, and see him for myself.'

Breathing Prayer

Wash me, Lord Jesus.

Prayer

I would have felt just as Peter did Lord, seeing you
kneeling at my feet. I too would have thought that
this was the wrong way round. Perhaps my
commitment to you does not measure up to his
fierce love, although I wish it did. But I am truly one
of your disciples and I want You to do for me what-
ever it takes to help me stay that way. Work your
will with me as You did with Peter, Lord, and may you
find me willing clay in the Potter's loving hands.

Amen.

Jesus got up from the meal, took off his outer clothing, and wrapped a towel round his waist. After that, he poured water into a basin and began to wash his disciples' feet, drying them with the towel that was wrapped round him. **John 13: 4,5**

The upper room is filled with the shadows of evening. The house in which it is situated is high on a hill looking out over a steep slope to the craggy peaks beyond. The valley in between is bathed in the setting sun and full of the smoky glow of hundreds of camp fires.

The twelve disciples at the table are quietly talking together, when Jesus gets up, and with all eyes on Him, takes off His outer robe, wraps a large towel round His waist and with a bowl of water begins to wash and dry the disciples' feet. Silence falls on the room as one by one each man's feet are washed and dried.

At last Jesus comes to Peter. He kneels at his feet and reaches out a hand to guide his feet into the bowl. 'Never, at any time will you wash my feet, Lord,' declares Peter in emphatic tones. Quietly Jesus looks up into Peter's face, seeing deep into his troubled spirit. Gently He says 'If I do not wash your feet, you will no longer be my disciple, Peter.'

What terrible words were these? They hit Peter like a blow in the face. He bursts out before He can stop himself, 'Lord, do not wash only my feet, then! Wash my hands and head too!' Quietly Jesus reassures the frightened disciple. He then takes off the wet towel, puts on His outer garment again and sits down at the table once more. With all eyes turned on Him, He explains what he has done. 'I, your Lord and Teacher, have just washed your feet. You, then, should wash one another's feet.'

Breathing Prayer

Fill me, living water.

Prayer

What a beautiful picture of your infilling Holy Spirit,
this life-giving stream makes Lord Jesus, and what a
contrast to a stagnant, dead pool. Yet for the stream
to run through it the stream bed has to give it room.
Help me to give your Spirit free passage in my life so
that I may come alive as It washes over me with
your Love.

Amen.

Whoever believes in me, as the Scripture has said, streams of living water will flow from within him.
John 7:38

Walking in the hills one day, you come across a muddy pool. It is evil-smelling, covered in scum and devoid of life. No animals appear to drink its water and it is fast shrinking under the rays of the Summer sun.

In sharp contrast you next stumble upon a mountain stream tumbling and leaping its joyful way down to the valley. The water is crystal clear and the steam is fringed with grass and flowers. You follow along its banks. Gradually the slope of the hill levels out and the stream becomes more sedate. Occasionally it broadens out into clear, slow-moving pools where trout and stickleback swim and the 'shy-eyed' delicate deer come down in a troupe to drink.

Here the stream is fringed by willows and alders and along its bank in marshy places grow kingcups and watercress, all drawing life, even in the hottest season, from its water.

Occasionally you see other signs of life. In one place an otter's head momentarily breaks the surface of the water, and holes under the bank show where water voles live. Quietly rounding a bend you see a flash of blue feathers as a kingfisher skims down off a leafy perch to catch up on unsuspecting fish.

You find a hollow along the bank where you lie down and rest. Closing your eyes you are aware of the fragrant scent of crushed wild thyme and the sounds made by the cattle near by as they munch away at the grass. The sun is warm on your face and the sound of the stream forms a beautiful background to your quiet contentment. The last thing you hear before you fall asleep is the singing of a lark high up in the heavens, the notes of its song falling round you like liquid sunbeams.

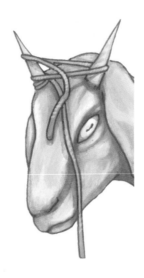

Breathing Prayer
Forgive my sins, Lord Jesus.

Prayer
How relieved the Israelites must have felt that there
was some way in which they could get rid of their
sins Lord, and how good that they could actually see
this ritual acted before their eyes. But I want to
thank you Lord that I don't need this Old Testament
symbolism to take away my sins on a yearly basis, but
have your once-and-for-all sacrifice on the cross to
do the same for me. Help me never to get used to
the immensity of your sacrifice.

Amen.

He is to lay both hands on the head of the live goat and confess over it all the wickedness and rebellion of the Israelites - all their sins - and put them on the goat's head. He shall send the goat away into the desert.

Leviticus 16:21

Imagine that you are standing in the sandals of one of the children of Israel on their journey to the promised land. It's the day of Atonement. All around you is the vast, tented camp of your fellow countrymen, set out in orderly blocks. In the centre of the camp is what looks a bit like a portacabin covered over with skins. This is the Tabernacle. Around the Tabernacle is a courtyard with walls made out of material.

Today this courtyard is full of people and there are also people all round the outside of the enclosure. In front of the Tabernacle, by an altar and a vast bronze bowl full of water, stands Aaron, the high priest, dressed in embroidered robes of white and blue and gold. On his head is a tall hat also white and blue and gold.

A goat with a scarlet rope twined in its horns stands in front of Aaron. He places both hands on the goat's head and in a loud voice, so that even those outside the enclosure can hear, he recites all the sins you and your fellow Israelites have committed over the last year.

Then a man steps forward, catches hold of the scarlet rope and leads the goat away. A path opens for them as they pass out of the Tabernacle precincts, through the outer throng and away to the edge of the camp. All eyes follow them until they are two small specks resolutely journeying towards the far reaches of the inhospitable wilderness.

A collective sigh goes up as the weight of last year's sins falls from each person present.

Breathing Prayer

I trust you Lord Jesus.

Prayer

There are so many things Lord Jesus which would
try to come in between me and my love for you. My
job, my situation, my family. Also the sorrows of life
and the problems I face. They, like Judas, seek to
destroy my peace and my confidence that I am doing
the right thing. Please help me, when my tranquility
is threatened, to hear the words of support and
affirmation. Thank you Lord Jesus for being on my
side.

Amen.

Then Mary took about a pint of pure nard, an expensive perfume; she poured it on Jesus' feet and wiped his feet with her hair. And the house was filled with the fragrance of the perfume.
John 12:3

Imagine that you are standing by an open window at a house in Bethany just before the first Easter. The view out of the window is a spectacular vista, looking down a steep valley to the far away wilderness. The sides of the valley are covered with grass and flowers.

The room behind you seems to be full of people and you turn to see a feast in progress. Around a triclinium are reclining about a dozen or so men. On the table are the remains of the feast, bowls of fruit and nuts, figs and dates. Suddenly you become aware of a most beautiful smell. You glance to your left and see that crouching behind the guest in the place of honour is a woman. The guest is Jesus, and the woman Mary. She has just broken the top off an expensive container of perfume and poured the contents all over Jesus' feet.

Not only the room is filled with the beautiful scent, but the fragrance seeps into every part of the house. Faces appear at the doorway to the room to see what is going on. A hush falls on the company as they realise the love and devotion that go into this act, and see the look of worship Mary gives to Jesus.

Then a harsh voice shatters the silence. It is Judas. 'Why wasn't this perfume sold and the money given to the poor?' he asks. The beautiful moment is spoiled. Destroyed like a smashed vase. Then Jesus speaks. 'Leave her alone' he says. 'Let her keep what she has for the day of my burial.' And somehow the moment is saved and repaired, and peace comes again.

A triclinium.

Breathing Prayer
Shed for me.

Prayer
At the most solemn and wonderful meal of all times,
Lord, you used simple things such as bread and wine,
which had grown in the fields and vineyards of your
native country, and gave them eternal significance.
May I use the ordinary things of my life, those things
which may seem dull and commonplace,
for your glory.

Amen.

In the same way, after the supper he took the cup, saying, 'This cup is the new covenant in my blood.'
Luke 22:20

You are standing in the wide, mountain-bordered plain of Jezreel. All around you stretch the vines, apparently sere and dead. As you watch you see life begin to stir. Little leaves appear and unfurl themselves, clothing the vines in green beauty. Bunches of green grapes, gradually ripen as the hot sun transforms them into glorious purple.

As you gaze at one particularly large bunch, a brown hand reaches out and picks it. You turn to see a worker in eastern dress putting the bunch into a basket already full of grapes. You follow him as he walks through the vineyard to the wine press, where he tips his load to join countless others.

Amid cheerful shouts of laughter and song the grapes are trodden, and the dark juices flow into the reservoir. You watch carefully as the wine is strained and then put in new wine skins. Not bottles, for this is circa AD 28 not the 20th century.

The skins are loaded onto donkeys and you go with them on their journey, up to the holy city of Jerusalem. From the flat plains you eventually climb up and up through the Judean hills until the sight of the Golden Temple tells you that you have arrived.

Your wine is unloaded and sold in one of the markets to what appear to be simple fishermen, but are really Jesus' disciples, perhaps Peter or even Judas. Then you see the skin carefully carried to the house with the upper room. Once there it is decanted into earthenware pitchers and put on the table for the last supper. Quietly, carefully, at the appropriate time, Jesus pours the wine out which you have watched grow and says those never-to-be-forgotten words, 'This is my blood shed for you.'

Breathing prayer

You have forgiven my sins.

Prayer

I can't bend my mind to imagine the breadth and
length of the Universe, Lord Jesus. I find it hard to
imagine going to Australia let alone deep space. But
You know it. You are as at home there as I am in my
back garden. And it is enough for me to know that
you have removed my sin and guilt and made me
once again free and joyful and full of gratitude.
Thank you.

Amen.

Imagine for yourself a flying machine. Make it comfortable and attractive. You are going to take your forgiven sins as far away as you possibly can on earth.

When you commence your journey the countryside below you looks familiar, fields, and houses and little towns. And then the sea, blue and sparkling in the sun passes underneath. Imagine all the other sights you would see. Vast plains baking in the hot sun, with herds of wild game roaming across them. High mountain ranges, covered with snow leading down into sheltered valleys. Huge cities which seem to go on forever as you fly over sprawling suburbs. Perhaps wild deserts where only the sand and the rock seem real. And then sea again, endless miles of it with tiny boats which look like toys.

You set your machine down somewhere, maybe on a high alpine pasture and savour the pure keen air and the view of snow-covered peaks.

When you have got as far away as you can you leave your sins and return home. Maybe you sleep or perhaps look at the unrolling vista below as you journey home.

It's just possible however, that the text may refer not to distances on earth but to space. Maybe God has removed our sins to the outermost reaches of the Galaxy. Here you cannot journey, but have to imagine the distances. To see in your mind's eye the sight of earth as it appears from space. And then to watch it receding as the distance lengthens until the other planets are passed. Then out into unknown deep space, past undiscovered stars and galaxies until your sins arrive at the very edge of the universe. So far has He removed our transgressions from us.

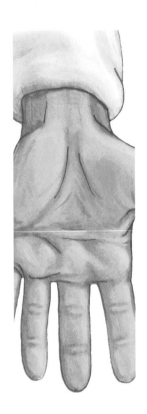

Breathing Prayer

Safe in your hand.

Prayer

I am astonished to know Lord God that you have
engraved my name on the palm of your hand. The
way I often treat you, I would think you would want
to forget it, not have it indelibly before your face, for
all eternity. You really must love me. I can't being to
understand your love but I can begin to enjoy the
feeling of security that it gives me, and to
praise You for it.

Amen.

See, I have engraved you on the palms of my hands; your walls are ever before me.
Isaiah 49:16

Either in reality or in imagination, look at your curled up hand. Slowly uncurl the fingers and look carefully at what you see. It may be that you have never really looked at your own hand before. Trace the lines on your palm and notice how cleverly God has placed the thumb in relation to the fingers.

Remember some of the things your hand has done for you today. The things you have made, the words you have written or typed, the people whom this hand has brought comfort and love. Perhaps your hand has cared for little children or old people and made them feel wanted and secure.

Now visualise another hand behind yours. This hand is bigger but is also in a curled up position. You sense that it is very strong and you can see the muscles near the wrist. You can also see that the finger ends are used to hard work. Yet it looks a creative hand, an artistic one. It looks, too, to be the sort of hand you would like to have near you in a crisis or if anything needed to be mended that had gone wrong. A hand to be trusted and welcomed.

Gradually the fingers begin to uncurl and the hand is revealed in all its strength. This is no ordinary hand you see, but the hand of God. And then, as the little finger, the last to uncurl, straightens, you notice that there is something written across the palm of the hand, and wonderingly, you read your own name -----------------. Gently you hear God saying to you, 'Yes, my child, I love you so much that I have written your own precious name on the palm of my hand for ever. I will never forget you. You are always in my mind and I am always planning for your good.' Quietly you rest in the knowledge that you really do matter to the God who made the universe.

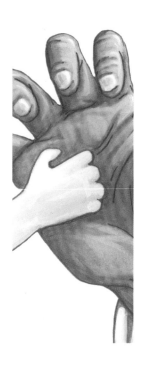

Breathing Prayer

I trust you great God.

Prayer

Nobody, Lord, could say that Isaac's birth was a
fortunate accident. There was nothing else it could
have been but an out and out miracle. And it is still
as miraculous today as it was then. Help me to
praise and thank you for it, even tho' it happened so
long ago, and to remember that you are the great 'I
am' whose power is the same in the past , the
present and the future.

Amen.

*He [God] took him [Abraham] outside and said,
'Look up at the heavens and count the stars - if
indeed you can count them.' Then he said to him,
'So shall your offspring be.'*
Genesis 15:5
*[The story of Abraham can be found in the early chapters of
Genesis.]*

You are observing a man sitting on a pile of rugs in a
Bedouin tent. He is old. A hundred years old to be
precise and he is expectantly waiting for something.
The tent entrance curtain is pulled aside and a woman
enters with a bundle held carefully in her arms. The
man, Abraham, rises to meet her and bending over a
bundle gently parts it to reveal a newborn baby fast
asleep, tired out with his arduous passage into the
world. You mark the look of wonder on his face as he
gazes at Sarah's son, Sarah his wife, who is ninety years
old. All these years he has waited and trusted God
even when it seemed that it was utterly impossible for a
baby to be born, and yet here he is, little Isaac.

Tenderly he lifts the baby's tiny hand, and lays it on his
big one. The baby's hand is so small and soft and vul-
nerable, and Abraham's hand so large and gnarled and
old. 'How' wonders Abraham 'can this tiny little
creature become as numerous as the stars in the sky
and the sand on the sea shore?' And yet surely, God,
who has performed the miracle of bringing Isaac
out of the deadness of his parent's bodies can do
even that.

His mind seems to range over the future millenia
and he sees myriads of people, his people, there
in the ages to come.

The baby sighs and opens its eyes and Abraham,
for the first time, looks with love into the face of
God's promised son.

Breathing Prayer

You hold my hand.

Prayer

Parents take infinite care over their children. Even so
our heavenly Father takes infinite pains over me, his
child. You want the best for me Lord God, and you
have continuously encouraged me all through my life
to find and develop those skills you gave me at my
birth. I like to think of you being joyful, like that
earthly father, when I succeed. And when I fail, gently
and firmly setting me back on my feet and helping
me to try again.

Amen.

Yet I was the one who taught Israel to walk. I took my people up in my arms, but they did not acknowledge that I took care of them.

Hosea 11:3

DAY TWENTY-SEVEN

A mother and father are teaching their eighteen-month-old baby son to walk. Mum is on one side of the room and Dad the other. Mum puts baby on his feet where he stands swaying, fighting for balance. When he seems stable, Dad, who has been standing smiling at his son and encouraging him, holds out his arms and says 'Come to Daddy.'

The little boy starts his faltering progress across the room. In the middle, he wavers and sits down hard on his bottom. Mum and Dad exclaim but don't rush to pick him up. knowing that a few tumbles are inevitable if he is ever to learn to walk. With more words of encouragement he scrambles to his feet, gets his balance and starts off again towards Dad.

Dad stretches out his arms and again saying 'Come to Daddy.' His face full of love, encouragement and welcome. With bated breath the parents watch as their son takes the last few steps which separate him from his father, and then Dad catches him up in his arms and swings him round. 'You're Daddy's clever boy' he cries to him.

The little boy is so thrilled with his achievement that he laughs and chuckles and treats the whole incident as one of life's great joyous experiences.

Dad then sets him down on his feet, and this time it is mother who calls to him and Father who sets him off on another epic journey.

Later in the day, Father and son can be seen walking round the garden, with son's hand firmly in Dad's and Dad again encouraging him to walk up and down the path, without sitting.

Breathing Prayer

Jesus, with me.

Prayer

It's hard for me to enter into the overwhelming joy
of the disciples, Lord, when they saw you, raised
from the dead. How astonished they must have
been when You ate that fish, and when the bolder
ones touched your warm, living resurrection body, a
thrill of pure joy must have coursed through them.
Help me to look forward to the same glorious
experience in heaven, when I too will see Jesus, in an
even more wonderful meeting than they had.

Amen.

While they were still talking about this, Jesus himself stood among them and said to them, 'Peace be with you.'
Luke 24:36

The scene is a room in Jerusalem late at night. A meal has just been eaten and the flickering light of the lamps catches the twinkling eyes of the discarded fish heads still on the plates. An excited group of disciples and other followers are listening eagerly as the two from Emmaus tell of Jesus' appearance to them. [Luke 24]

Suddenly everyone is aware that there is a difference in the room. They turn to look, and there is Jesus. 'Peace be with you' he says. They clutch at each other and you can feel their terror at this fantastic sight. 'There's nothing to be afraid of' says Jesus. 'It really is me. Look, at the wounds in my hands.' And he holds His hands out for them all to see. "Feel me. I am not a ghost, but a real being, with bones and flesh.' Even so the group is still hesitant and fear is still written on all faces although, here and there, smiles begin to peep out like sunbeams from behind clouds.

"Come now,' says Jesus, 'Just to prove I am no ghost, give me something to eat.' Several people look round the room, and one notices a bit of fish still on a plate. Carefully he hands the plate to Jesus, who takes the fish and eats it in front of them. As he swallows the last mouthful, a sigh goes up from the group and their joy and wonder is incredible to watch.

Then quietly Jesus sits down in the middle of the group. Some of the disciples sit round him and some stand for a better view, whilst the most amazing Bible Study begins as Jesus explains to them the reason for His death and Resurrection. 'You must wait' He concludes, 'here, in Jerusalem, until the power of the Holy Spirit is given you.' There is complete silence as all hang on His every word.

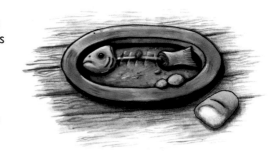

Breathing Prayer

White and clean and perfect.

Prayer

There are so many images for purity Lord and none
of them adequately expresses the reality. I find it
hard to understand how all my sins can be there one
minute and the next it's as if they had never been.
But I trust you Lord and I hope to spend eternity
showing You how grateful I am that you have done
this for me.

Amen.

'Come now, let us reason together,' says the Lord. 'Though yours sins are like scarlet, they shall be as white as snow.'
Isaiah 1:18

DAY TWENTY-NINE

You are standing in a beautiful, old, walled garden. There are green grassy walks, herbaceous borders and fruit trees everywhere. The borders have been planted with flowers in pastel shades of blue, pink and yellow, which give a mellow tranquil effect. That is, all except a large rambler rose on one of the walls, which is bright scarlet.

You walk to the rose, and look at it. It is covered with a profusion of blooms of such an intensity of vermilion that it makes your eyes hurt to see it. It's brash and bold and loud in complete contrast to the other gentle flowers in the garden.

A brief shower falls and you take shelter in a Summer house. After the rain has ceased, you return and once more look at the rose. To your amazement, as you watch, the hectic crimson begins to fade. You blink. Are you imagining things? But no. It really is beginning to diminish, first to rouge, then deep pink and little by little through all shades to the palest blush and eventually to pure white.

Each bloom is now of the colour of fresh snow, cool and unsullied, like flowers from that first garden where all was perfect and original. You are impressed by how beautiful the effect of the massed white blooms is and how it makes a united whole with the other flowers in the garden. Then the sun comes out and each rose not only glows with purest white but sparkles as the light catches the limpid rain drops caught up in its petals. Even so the soul, which has been purified by the crimson love of the Son.

Breathing Prayer

Praise You, praise You, Father God.

Prayer

The world you have made for me, Father, is
wonderful, beautiful, and full of tghings to sustain me.
Most of the time I don't notice it as my eyes are on
my work and myself. I miss the praises of Your
creation and am infinitely the poorer for doing so.
Tune me in, Lord, to the song of Your world, so that
we may praise You together in deep harmony.

Amen.

You fill the streams with water; you provide the earth with crops. This is how you do it——. Everything shouts and sings for joy.
Psalm 65:9 13

You are standing by the side of a ploughed field. It has been raining and there is a beautiful smell of wet earth in the air. As you watch you see little blades of wheat come pushing through the earth until the field is covered with their ordered rows.

The air becomes warmer and more Spring-like and the little plants grow fast until there is a sea of green where once there was only the shining brown of the wet earth. You are aware of the warmth of the sun and the song of birds. You sit under the shade of an ash tree at the field's edge and watch as the green wheat begins to ripen. Slowly the whole field changes from green to glowing yellow. A light breeze blows and ripples across the golden sea sighing and catching up a lark's song as it drifts past.

Across the hedge are pastures, sweeping upwards to follow line of wooded hills. These are covered with sheep and plump lambs, grazing lazily in the Summer sun.

The whole scene is one of abundance and tranquility. Somehow it seems as if the countryside has a life of its own, and that it is rejoicing in what God has caused it to produce. As you listen you can hear the melody of its praises. Deep notes from the tranquil wooded hillsides, gentle harmony from the fields full of sheep and lambs, and above all the bright, clear praise of the shining golden corn. You joint his symphony of rejoicing in the goodness and providence of your Father God.